His Divine Presence

Dennis J. Billy, C.Ss.R.

En Route Books and Media, LLC
Saint Louis, MO

⊕*ENROUTE*
Make the time

En Route Books and Media, LLC

5705 Rhodes Avenue

St. Louis, MO 63109

contact@enroutebooksandmedia.com

Cover Credit: Sebastian Mahfood

Copyright 2022 Dennis J. Billy, C.Ss.R.

ISBN-13: 978-1-956715-78-1

LCCN: 2022943366

For the poet in each of us

O come, let us sing to the Lord!

Psalm 95:1

Table of Contents

When the Day Comes

When the day comes that I breathe my last,
And bid farewell to this good earth,
To the life I have lived,
And the friends I have traveled with,
I hope those around me will find gratitude
In my eyes for what is past,
And a smile on my lips—
In expectant hope of what is still to come.

When the Darkness

When the darkness looms,
Be aware of my presence
And know that I am there.
When the rivers roar
And the oceans rage,
Reach for my hand
And know that I am near.
You must never despair.
You must never cease trusting.
I am here at your side.
I will never abandon you.
I will never leave you.
You are my beloved,
The apple of my eye.
All that I have is yours—
And so very much more.

When Distant Mountains

When distant mountains appear on the horizon
And bid me climb their soaring heights,
When earth pierces sky, and rock
Meets air in its rarified state,
When inspiration discards the need for comfort
And bids the heart to yearn for something more,
When courage lacks strength, and strength then
Seeks a deeper well from which to draw,
Only then will I depart and allow
The journey to take me where it will,
Only then will I set out on an adventure
From which there is no return.
Such mountain peaks, I know, are beyond
My meager means, but journey there I must,
Trusting in the belief I do not sojourn alone,
That in the loneliness of my walk
A silent companion accompanies me,
Who has traveled to these distant peaks,
And those far beyond them—
Many, many times before.

The Journey

This is not our homeland:
We are all wayfarers,
Pilgrims on a quest,
In search of a deeper truth
That ever evades
And eludes us in our search.
Yet still we travel,
It's in our blood,
Travelers are we,
Travelers we were meant to be,
Travelers we will ever be,
Travelers who live for the journey,
As the journey lives for us,
And becomes us,
And cannot be parted from us.

The Eternal Silence

I listen to the silence
Beneath the spoken word.
It is a gentle silence—
Quiet and unobtrusive—
One that speaks by listening,
And listens by its being present
To the momentary pause
In a conversation,
To a concealed thought
Yet to see the light of day,
To the hidden smile,
To the blink of an eye,
To the rhythm of a heartbeat,
And to the lonely, existential sigh
That marks our harrowing sojourn
Into the Eternal Silence
That calls us from within
And beckons us Home.

The Day Will Come

The day will come when tears will disappear,
And slowly sadness also dissipate.
Depression, too, won't want to us draw near,
And melancholy's gait will hesitate.
The day will come when all that's wrong in Life
Will slip away and let the Sun shine through.
The day will come when there will be no strife,
And Light will Light the way to what is True.

The Coming of Day

The day will come when sorrow will leave this land,
When darkness will flee approaching dawn,
And light will cast out shadows from our midst.
The day will come when emptiness will cease,
When yearning will wrestle unseen treasures,
And death discover life's hidden bliss.
The day will come when light itself will flee,
When time and space will yield eternity,
And shield our weary eyes from the bright unveiling.
Yes, the day will come, when what is not seen will be seen,
And what is seen will turn to darkness,
And what is dark will give way to light,
And what is light will cease to shine.
Ever near, yet ever far, that day, even now we see
In the dreams that wake us in the night,
And give us hope for the coming of day.

The Approaching Dawn

When darkness falls and night descends
Upon the remnants of day,
When the sun sinks beneath the horizon
And carries its light to distant shores,
When the stars awake from sleep
And cover the sky with silent wonder,
When the moon shines upon the soul
And helps it find its deep, cratered landscape,
I hope I will bow my head in gratitude
For the end of day, the utter stillness of life,
And the stirring in my heart, each and every night,
Of the lingering shadow of the approaching dawn.

As the Years Pass

As the years pass,
And as I grow old,
As evening draws near,
And I face my final hour,
I ask myself
When looking back,
"What meaning did
I find in Life:
For what purpose
Did I live?
An answer came
In the silence of my heart
In the quiet stillness,
Which told me this:
"To live each day
As though it were my last
And to cherish each moment
As if it were eternity."

Every Present Moment

When the time comes for me to say what I think
And not what those around me wish to hear,
When the time comes for me to be honest with myself
And reveal to others the truth that needs telling,
When the time comes for me to stand up for what I believe,
Regardless of the consequences and what others may think,
I hope I have the courage then to follow my convictions,
And the wherewithal to find that strength in every present moment.

Forging a Path

I am forging a path
Of my own making.
Where it will lead
I do not know.
Nor do I wish to know.
Part of the adventure of Life
Is in navigating the darkness
Of not knowing.
Part of its challenge
Is in plumbing
The depths of uncertainty
And finding one's deeper self
In the process.

Gratitude

Whenever I encounter loss
Or hardship,
Whenever things don't
Fall into place,
And Life's downward pull
Seems to have
The upper hand,
I think of all
The good things
I have
And have been
Blessed with
In my Life.

All of which
Have been given
To me without
My asking.
I ponder them,
Remember them
And embrace them,
As I smile,
Close my eyes,

His Divine Presence

Bow my head
In silence
And send
A heartfelt prayer
To God
In gratitude.

His Divine Presence

His Divine Presence
Is everywhere:
In the beauty of creation,
In the stars that shine,
In the flowers that spring,
In the trees that bend,
In the leaves that fall,
In the birds that sing,
In the paths we walk,
In the mountains we climb,
In the rivers we travel,
In the oceans we cross,
In the love we give,
In the families we form,
In the friendships we share,
In the communities we shape,
In the food we eat,
In the homes we build,
In the work we do,
In the play we make,
In the music we sing,
In the letters we write,
In the births we see,

His Divine Presence

In the lives we live,
In the crosses we bear,
In the troubles we find,
In the hearts we mend,
In the deaths we face,
In the happiness we seek,
In the faith we hold,
In the churches we fill,
In the world we serve,
In the poor we meet,
In the saints we honor,
In the Word we proclaim,
In the Masses we celebrate,
In the Bread we eat,
In the Wine we drink,
In the worship we render
Unto God, who created us,
The universe, and all things in it,
Who is the Alpha and the Omega,
The Beginning and the End,
And who lives and reigns
Forever and ever—
Amen!

Into the Dawn

In the dead of night,
I opened my eyes,
Arising from a deep sleep,
Not knowing where I was
Or from where
I had come.
Not knowing,
Simply not knowing.

I breathed in
The enveloping Darkness.
As it filled my lungs,
I felt as though
It had cut through
The marrow of my bones
And penetrated
My entire Being.

I felt alone in all the Universe,
Empty, lost, and without purpose.
I did not know where I was,
Or where I was going.
Unnerved by the surrounding stillness,

His Divine Presence

I peered into the night, listened,
And for a moment,
Thought I heard the Darkness speak.

"Listen," it said, "Listen to me.
Do not be afraid. You are not alone.
Walk with me. Befriend me.
Trust me. Follow me.
I am not the absence of Light,
But its necessary complement.
The path I follow
Leads directly to the Dawn."

Icon

I contemplate the image before me
And peer into the beyond.
Image and symbol juxtaposed
Reveal another dimension
Of time and space
That peers into my world
And gives back to me
A glimpse of eternity.

A Walk at Dusk

As the sun goes down,
My thoughts grow quiet.
I ponder the beauty of the moment,
As Nature welcomes the darkness
And cools itself from the heat of the day.
I breathe in the cool air
And let it out, as if in a prayer.
Wonder fills my heart— with solitude.
I smile at the sun, welcome
The moon and its gentle light,
And return from my walk
A grateful and contented man.

Beyond

Look beyond the sky,
Beyond the sun,
Beyond the stars and planets,
Beyond the boundaries of space and time,
Beyond what you can see,
Beyond what you can imagine,
Beyond your highest hopes,
Beyond your deepest dreams.

What do you see in that beyond?
What do you not see?
What lies hidden from you
Above the beyond?
Below the beyond?
Beside the beyond?
Beyond the beyond
Deep within your soul?

His Divine Presence

A Hymn of Praise

Praise be to You, God, Our Father,
Creator of the world we travel in!
Praise be to You, Jesus, the Word Incarnate,
Redeemer of the World and Victor over Death!
Praise be to You, Holy Spirit, the Comforter,
Who sanctifies us and dwells within our hearts!
Praise be to you, Most Holy Trinity,
In Whom we live, and move, and have our being!

A Different Day

Our days are numbered,
Each and every one of them.
We cannot add
A single day,
Or hour,
Or moment
To our lives.
Yet live we must
With the endless march of Time,
The finitude of Life,
The certainty of Death,
And the quiet hope
That we will live to see
The Rising Sun of another day.

Come, Lord Jesus!

From his mother's womb
To the womb of a darkened cave,
A child is born, bringing Light
To a darkened world,
A helpless child
Sent to a helpless world
To heal it of its wounds
And bring it back to Life.

Come, Lord Jesus, come!
Cry out in the cold of night
From the warmth
Of your swaddling clothes!
Rest in the hay of the manger
Where the animals feed!
Live among us
So we might live with you!

Emmanuel, God with us,
Come, stay with us!
Come to us in this dark of night!
Become our food, our rest, our hope,
Our deepest yearning!
In this our darkest hour
In this our time of need,
Come, Lord Jesus, come!

The Lives We Live

We and the journey
Are intertwined,
Becoming one,
Never ending,
Ever eluding,
Forever challenging,
Always leading,
Always looking,
Always seeking
The journey's end
And where it
Will lead us.
This is what
We look forward to.
This is why
We live in hope.
This is why we journey.
This is why we live
The lives we live.

The Night Sky

Looking up at the night sky,
Pondering the moon,
Reveling in the stars,
Contemplating the magnitude
Of space and time,
I feel so unimportant,
So small,
So insignificant.

But then, a simple thought
Crosses my mind:
All of this,
All that is before me,
All that I can see
And have yet to see,
Was made for me,
One day to behold.

The Other Side

Journey to the still of now,
Beneath the turbulence of when,
Before the placement of where,
The naming of who,
The question of what,
The end of how,
Or the look of why.

Go there,
Without a care,
Without a sigh,
To lie in the solitude of not,
To pull back the veil of then,
And discover in the empty void,
The other side of you.

The Present Moment

Live in the present moment.
Welcome each one,
As if it were the only one.
Taste it.
Savor it.
Be one with it.
Let it come.
Then let it go.
Mourn its passing.
Rejoice in its rebirth.
Proclaim it freshness.
Ponder its stillness.
Listen to its silence.
Let it take you by surprise.
Let it romance you,
Befriend you,
Entertain you,
Quiet you.
Let it help you
Peer into eternity's
Timeless gaze
And rest in the tranquil peace
Of the here and now.

The Depth of Things

Do not live
On the surface
Of things.
Go beneath them.
Embrace them.
Savor them.
Taste them.
Invite them
Into yourself.
Welcome them.
Caress them.
Revere them.
Become them.
Dare to delve
Beneath
What eye
Can see.
Behold what
Is there
And not
There.
Live life
At its depth,
And the depth

His Divine Presence

Of life
Will breathe
In you
An ever deeper
Longing
For the ground,
The source,
The fountain
From which
All things
Flow…

His Divine Presence

Grace

Did you ever
Wish you were
Never born
Because Life
Has beaten
You down
So badly,
And there seems
No reason
For Living?
I have,
And so have
Many others.

Life's downward pull
Has a way
Of smothering us
With negativity.
Don't let it do
To you
What it has done
To me
And so many others!
Resist

His Divine Presence

While you can!
Seek a deeper help!
Pray!

Life's downward pull
Is itself
An illusion.
One day
It too will fall,
One day,
Its weak and shallow
Pull will give way
To a deeper,
Much gentler,
Upward force,
Which goes by the name
Of "Grace."

The Break of Day

A wonderful grace,
The gift of Life,
So fragile in every way.
Senseless the act
That brings it Death
Before the break of day.

Acedia

There is a downward pull in Life
That depresses the heart,
Numbs the soul,
And leads to melancholy.
When under its spell
Time stands still,
Space implodes,
And paralysis reigns.
Unable to live Life
As it wishes
And needs to be lived,
We turn in upon ourselves
Lick our wounds,
Feel sorry for ourselves,
Regret the day we were born,
And curse the womb that bore us.
Asleep in sleep,
Numbed by our own self-pity,
We medicate ourselves into oblivion,
As we anticipate the end of the day
And yearn for the coming of night.

Stranger

I need to know
If you will be there
In time of need,
Or simply fade away
With the passage of time
To become a mere memory,
A once valued friend,
But now someone
I know not—
A stranger to me,
And I to you.

Remember Me

Remember me at the setting of the sun,
When the last rays of day depart,
And the moon's reflected light heralds night.
Remember me when the stars appear
And edify the darkness with their distant beauty
That quiets the mind and heightens our inner yearning.
Remember me when darkness descends
And covers the earth with its tranquilizing blanket of sleep,
Calling each to each and each to unconscious hope.
Remember me, there, in that special place, and I will you.
When the day is done, the time for dreaming is at hand.

Wonder

Did you ever wonder
Why the sun rises,
The seasons change,
The leaves fall,
The showers pour,
The snow drifts,
The flowers bloom,
The birds sing,
And the children play?
Did you ever wonder
Why there are
So many wonders
To behold
Each day
And every day
For the rest of your life
And then some?
I have.
Truth be told:
I wonder
At the sheer wonder
Of it all!
There is
So much to ponder

His Divine Presence

And behold
And relish,
So much
To be grateful
And thankful for!
Truth be told—
It is so very wonderful
To be alive!

My Words

My words are meaningless,
If I do not believe what they say.
They reveal my inner hypocrisy,
If they do not inspire action.
My words are entirely without meaning,
If they do not flow from the Word
Who gives meaning to Life,
And whose actions point out
The way to the Father.

Remember

Remember yesterday,
And the day before yesterday,
And the day before that,
And the day before that,
And the day before that!
Each day is different,
Each day, the same.
It's the person remembering
Who makes the difference.

What I Do Not Know

I seek what I do not know,
Yet wish to know.
I strive for knowing the unknown
And entering into its dark light.
I seek the darkness that is light
And the light that reveals itself in darkness.
I look for certainty in the midst of uncertainty
And uncertainty that reveals itself as Truth.
Such is the life I live
From moment to moment,
From day to day,
From month to month
And year to year,
From eternity to eternity.

The Teacher

I am called to open minds
To the deeper side of Life,
To help them peer beneath appearances
And see what reveals itself
To those who ponder it.
I do not wish to impose,
Only propose,
And help those who listen
To see for themselves.

Silence

Listen to the silence
Within and without.
Allow its word of solitude
To take shape.
Let it still you
Quiet you,
And contemplate you.
Let it open your ears
And help you hear
The deep-down magic
Of every breath you draw
And every beat
Of your aching,
Yearning heart.

Another Day

What lies beyond the veil of Death,
On the other side of Life,
Have we, the generations, pondered,
And pondered,
And pondered again
And again—
But to no avail.

The answer lies shrouded in darkness
And cannot be penetrated by human thought;
Only a faint and ever so elusive ray of light
From the other side of death
Gives rest to our restless souls
And hope to our hearts—
For the coming of another day.

An Unmarked Trail

Take an unmarked trail
Of your own choosing
And follow it.
Walk along its winding path
Through the dark woods
Of an unknown landscape
To an open glade
In a strange location
Of unfamiliar surroundings,
Feeling lost in the midst
Of past decisions gone awry
And forgotten by everyone
Except yourself
And your image of yourself.
Walk for a while
But do not rush.
Take time to take things in.
Take a moment to relax.
The trail will be there
When you resume.
It will always be there
For you to wander
Through in fear,
Hidden anxiety,

His Divine Presence

Quiet solitude,
And unseen hope.
Stop and rest.
Allow time to stand still
For a moment or two.
Ponder the moment.
Rest in the shade
Of a nearby tree.
Take your shoes off.
Shield yourself
From the rays
Of the summer sun.
Stay there a while.
Enjoy the journey.
Contemplate your surroundings.
Open your eyes
To what is not seen.
Listen to the unheard.
Touch the grass beneath you.
Smell a flower's scent.

Courage

Courage confronts Fear
And refuses to
Be intimidated by it.
It sizes it up and seeks
To overcome it
In the light of
A greater Good.
It knows when to attack
And when to retreat.
It knows that Fear is
Nothing more
Than a ghastly Specter,
A hollow,
Fainting shadow
That despite
Its most tried
And valiant efforts
Cannot survive
The onslaughts
Of bravery
Dedicated to
The One
And Only
Good.

Dawn

Waning stars,
Fading darkness,
Night ending its day,
Birds chirping,
Trees breezing,
Leaves singing,
Daylight opening
Its eyes
To a red horizon
And a rising sun…

This Place

The time has come for me to leave this place,
And I wonder if I shall ever return,
(Not that I wouldn't like to if opportunity knocked).
Soon this present moment will become a faded memory,
An image sealed in my mind of events
That once was and never again shall be,
Of memories that will cross my mind from time to time,
Evoking a smile, a frown, or a tear,
(Depending on my mood and circumstance),
And leaving me to wonder, for better or worse,
About what was and what might have been,
About what could have been yet did not come to pass.
I leave this place with sadness in my heart,
With gratitude for the time spent here,
And with reverence for its quiet beauty,
Thankful for its impact on my life—
And the part of me I have left behind.

The Gift of Listening

Empty yourself of your inner noise.
Focus on the person before you.
Be present to him or her.
Ponder the words you hear.
Savor the silence between them.
Rest in the stillness beneath the words.
Then tell the person what you have heard.
Give him or her the gift of listening.

Faces

Everyone has
A public face,
A private face,
And a secret face.
Which mask
Are you wearing
At any given time,
And which one
Have you become?

Eucharist

The bread of which we now partake and eat
Becomes, for us, His flesh, the dream complete
Of Him who for Himself so long ago
Created us in Love, His Love to sow,
That every human heart might welcome Him,
However dim the light that burns within.

So gather we around His table now
From far and wide to genuflect and bow
Before this humble fare, this gift God sends,
This hidden presence given us that mends
Whatever shame we share from Adam's fall,
To rise with Him from death— the hope of all.

A Friend

A friend is someone you can turn to in need,
Someone who knows you, who seeks your well-being,
Someone who looks after you, as you look after him (or her),
Someone who is a kindred spirit, another soul,
Another self, who lives in your heart,
And who does so without counting the cost.
A friend is someone who knows how to suffer with you,
And who knows that you would be willing to do the same,
Someone who will not allow evil to interfere with life,
And who will not allow life to interfere with death.
Someone who knows you and who enables
You to remain true to yourself.
Someone who sees you as you truly are,
Who accepts you as you are,
And who is willing to travel with you,
Wherever the road may lead,
Until you become your deepest, truest self.

I Know Not Where

I know not where the path
I walk will lead,
If it will bring me closer
To my dreams,
Or farther away.
Long ago I chose it
In the quiet of the day:
I walk alone,
In silence,
With hope
As my sole companion.

Beneath

Beneath my awareness
There is a part of me
I do not know
Yet long to discover.
I wish to befriend
This deeper self
And go wherever
It leads me.

I Remember

I remember the day
When I considered
Myself another self
And tried to converse
With this unknown
Side of me.
At first, I was a stranger
To this unknow presence,
But slowly,
Little by little,
Over time,
We became
The closest
And most intimate
Of friends.

Fear

Fear lurks in the shadows
And takes root in darkness.
Once it grabs hold of a mind,
It refuses to let go.
It paralyzes, controls,
Overwhelms, imprisons, and destroys.
It spreads like a contagion—
Invisible to the eye,
But so very visible to the soul.

I Wonder

I wonder where
The years have gone.
I look back
And see so many
That have passed.
I look forward
And wonder
How many more will come
Before looking back
And looking forward
Become one and the same.

In the Dark

In the dark of night
My dreams fall asleep
And carry me to consciousness.
I open my eyes
And sense the yearning
Of the approaching dawn.
I close my eyes and return
To my own inner yearning
For the passing of night
And the rising of a distant sun.

Look

Look before you.
Look behind you.
Look around you.
Look above you.
Look below you.
Look every which way,
However you wish
Or do not wish!
Everything changes
When you begin
To look within.

A Seed

A seed, planted in the ground,
Must lay dormant in the soil,
Receiving into itself
The pull of the Earth,
The wear of the Seasons,
The march of Time,
The call of Nature,
Becoming what it is not,
Yet must become,
Before it can open its eyes
To the warm swell
Of the Sun's life-giving,
Sustaining rays.

A Single Day

If a single day
Is as a thousand years
In the eyes of the Lord,
I wonder if
A single moment
Contains eternity
And eternity
A single moment?

This Moment

This moment is passing
And will never return.
I wish to savor it,
While it is here.
I wish to taste
And touch it,
Hear and smell it,
Feel and see it.
I wish to breathe it in
And breathe it out.
I wish to make it a part of me,
So that I can become a part of it
Before it fades away
And finds its way
Back to eternity.

Moving Forward

I disagree with you,
And you disagree with me.
Where do we go from here?

I'd like to have lunch with you
And listen to you.
Perhaps you would also listen to me.

And maybe we could find
Some common ground
To share with one another.

That is my hope.
That is my prayer
In these dark times…

Faith

Night has fallen and into darkness we
Close our eyes with hope of more to see
Than what the lack of sun reveals.
In faith we walk, our eyes the darkness seals,
An inner light shining beneath our doubts,
A burning candle reveals our whereabouts.

Disciple

You lead,

I follow…

You teach,

I follow…

You serve,

I follow…

You suffer,

I follow…

You bleed,

I follow…

You die,

I follow…

You rise,

I follow…

All by the

Grace of God…

The Journey Ahead

Let us go forth before the break of day,
Our fears behind us, to find the chosen way.
Let us seek the better part, whate're the naysayers say.
We have come to march and march we will this day!

The day lasts long, and much have we to learn
Before the sunlight fades, and we to dusk adjourn.
The hours pass, our hearts within us burn.
But day has come, and much must we discern.

The Search

A dark night wakens the soul,

Leading it to a stillness deep within,

A place where emptiness is full of presence,

Where presence is emptied of fullness,

And where fullness is always seeking more…

What Awaits Me

The path I walk
Winds every which way
And has left me
Lost and disoriented.
I cannot see
Beyond the bend
And know not
What awaits me.

The Voice Within

I took a lonely road by chance, then somehow wandered off.
The path I chose was very dark and got me very lost.
I looked around with hopeful heart in search of needed light.
Instead, I heard a silent voice that in the stillness cried.
"Be not afraid," I heard it say, "to follow where I lead.
This dreadful night will slowly pass and gain for you your sight."
I listened to that still, small voice but pondered it in fear:
"This looming darkness threatens me and shakes me to the bone!
If I walk blindly through this night, I fear to lose all hope,
And Life itself will shut its eyes and leave me in this night!"
"Not so," I heard the whispering sound, "Not so!" I heard it say.
"If you but trust the voice within, the darkness there will pass.
And you will find a way to walk in darkness to the light!"
The years have passed, and I have lived to see a ripe old age.
The voice's words stay with me still: "There is a light ahead!"
My journey's end draws near to me: I see it from afar!

The Future

I know not where
The path I follow leads,
Untraveled, it is,
Overgrown with brush and weeds.
I take each step
And leave each step behind
With no end in sight—
Whatever shall I find?

Hope

To yearn for the dawn in the dark of night,
To see through the worrisome fog,
To sniff for the end when the end is out of sight,
And raise one's head from the mire of the muddy bog.

I Live

I live in the present
As I look to the past
And step into the future.
Once there, I find
That the present
Has never left me
And the future
Has become my past.

www.ingramcontent.com/pod-product-compliance
Lightning Source LLC
Chambersburg PA
CBHW060141050426
42448CB00010B/2240